# SILICON

## A TRUE BOOK®

by

**Salvatore Tocci**

**Children's Press®**
A Division of Scholastic Inc.

New York  Toronto  London  Auckland  Sydney
Mexico City  New Delhi  Hong Kong
Danbury, Connecticut

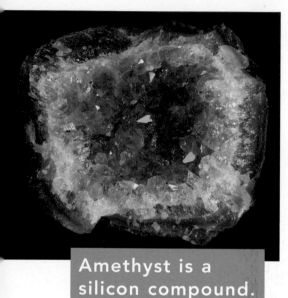

Amethyst is a silicon compound.

*Reading Consultant*
**Julia McKenzie Munemo, MEd**
*New York, New York*

*Science Consultant*
**John A. Benner**
*Austin, Texas*

*The photo on the cover shows silicon crystals. The photo on the title page shows pieces of silicon.*

*The author and the publisher are not responsible for injuries or accidents that occur during or from any experiments. Experiments should be conducted in the presence of or with the help of an adult. Any instructions of the experiments that require the use of sharp, hot, or other unsafe items should be conducted by or with the help of an adult.*

Library of Congress Cataloging-in-Publication Data

Tocci, Salvatore.
    Silicon / by Salvatore Tocci.
        p. cm. — (A true book)
    Includes bibliographical references and index.
    ISBN 0-516-23701-2 (lib. bdg.)    0-516-25577-0 (pbk.)
    1. Silicon—Juvenile literature. I. Title. II. Series.
QD181.S6T58 2005
546'.683—dc22                                              2004027153

# Contents

These fruits, called tangelos, are created when tangerines and grapefruits are combined.

# What Do You Call It?

Do you know the name of the fruits shown on the opposite page? You may think that they are oranges because of their color. Or you may have said that they are grapefruits because of their size and shape.

These fruits are neither oranges nor grapefruits. They

are tangelos, which are produced by crossing tangerines with grapefruits. Tangelos taste like tangerines but are about the size of grapefruits.

The name *tangelo* is a combination of two names. The *tange-* part of its name comes from tangerine. The *-lo* part of its name comes from pomelo. The pomelo is a large citrus fruit that is closely related to the grapefruit. The name tangelo indicates that this fruit has something in common with both a tangerine and a pomelo.

Some names used in science also indicate that a substance has something in common with two different things. An example can be seen with the **elements**. An element is a building block of **matter**. Matter is the stuff or material that makes up everything in the universe. This book, the chair you are sitting on, and even your body are all made of matter.

There are just a few more than one hundred different elements. Most of these elements conduct electricity. In other words, they allow electricity to pass through them easily. These elements are called metals. Some elements do not conduct electricity. These are called nonmetals.

There are some elements, however, that normally do not conduct electricity but can do

Gold is an example of an element that is a metal. The helium used to fill a balloon is an element that is a nonmetal.

so under the right conditions. In other words, sometimes these elements act like non-metals, and at other times they act like metals. So what are these elements called?

These elements are called **semiconductors**. The name semiconductor indicates that the element has something in common with both metals and nonmetals. Silicon is an example of an element that is a semiconductor.

# Where Is Silicon Found?

Silicon can be found almost everywhere. In fact, there is more silicon on Earth than any other element except one. The only element more common than silicon is oxygen. Silicon makes up slightly more than 25 percent of Earth's crust,

In addition to a name, every element also has a symbol. The symbol for silicon is *Si*.

which is the solid material that covers the planet's surface.

Even though silicon can be found almost everywhere, no matter how hard you search for it, you will not find it. Silicon does not exist by itself in nature. It is almost always found as part of a **compound**. A compound is a substance that is formed when two or more different elements are combined.

Although there are just slightly more than one hundred

elements, there are millions of different compounds. How can so many different compounds be made of so few elements?

Think about the English language. Just twenty-six letters can be arranged to make up all the words in the English language. Likewise, the one hundred elements can be arranged to make up millions of different kinds of compounds.

Silicon often combines with oxygen and other elements to form compounds known as **silicates**. Silicates are the most abundant minerals on Earth. The simplest silicates are compounds that are made of just silicon and oxygen. The silicon and oxygen can be arranged in many different ways to make up these compounds.

In some silicates, these two elements are arranged in

a random fashion. Sand is probably the most familiar example of such a silicate. In other silicates, the silicon and oxygen are arranged in a specific ordered pattern known as a **crystal**. One example is quartz. Quartz crystals come in many different sizes.

Another common silicate mineral is feldspar, which comes in different varieties. In fact, feldspar is the most common mineral on Earth.

Sand and quartz are examples of silicon compounds made of silicon and oxygen.

Depending on which elements are present, feldspars come in many colors, such as blue, white, and red.

Unlike sand and quartz, feldspar contains elements other than silicon and oxygen.

Other examples of silicate minerals include clay, granite, and asbestos. Like sand, quartz, and feldspar, these silicate minerals are also plentiful in Earth's crust. It's no wonder that you can find silicon almost anywhere you look.

# Absorbing Water

Cat litter is made almost entirely of clay, which is a silicate mineral. Clay absorbs water well. Find out which brand of cat litter absorbs water best. Use a needle to poke several holes in the bottom of a large paper cup. Fill the cup with litter. Next, fill a measuring cup with water. Hold the paper cup filled with litter over an empty bowl. Slowly pour the water into the litter. Measure how much water passes through the litter and into the bowl. Repeat this procedure using different brands of litter. The litter that absorbs the best is the one that allows the least amount of water to pass into the bowl.

# How Is Silicon Useful?

Of all the elements, silicon is one of the most useful because it is a semiconductor. Metals tend to get hot when they conduct electricity. In contrast, semiconductors do not. This property makes them useful for conducting

Crystals of pure silicon are flattened into little circles called wafers that are stamped to make computer chips.

electricity in devices such as transistors, light-emitting diodes (LEDs), and computer chips.

Although silicon is the element of choice for making computer chips, small amounts of other elements must be added to it. These elements increase silicon's ability to conduct electricity without getting hot.

Silicon compounds, such as silicates, are also very useful. Sand and clay are used to

A cement truck is loaded at a construction site.

make concrete and bricks.
Clay and feldspar are used
to make pottery.

Silicon compounds are used to make sandpaper.

A compound made of silicon and the element carbon is almost as hard as diamond.

This compound, called silicon carbide, is used to make sandpaper. Silicon carbide sandpaper is also known as "wet and dry" paper because it can be used to polish both wet and dry surfaces. Silicon carbide can be used to polish wood, ceramic, brass, aluminum, and glass.

One of the largest uses of a silicon compound is the use of certain kinds of sand for making glass. Glassmaking

A glassblower works with liquid glass.

has a very long history. Just where and when it started is not known. Glassmaking may have first started about five thousand years ago in either Asia or Egypt. One historian reports that soon after a group of sailors landed on a beach, they started a fire to cook their food. They were surprised to see the sand below the fire melting. As the sand melted, it formed a stream of liquid that slowly cooled and turned into glass.

Silicon is also considered an essential trace element. This means that we need a tiny amount of silicon to keep our bodies healthy. But the body can't make silicon so we must get it from foods. Silicon is present in onions, wheat, rice, green vegetables, and potatoes. Scientists have not established just how much silicon the body needs. The body appears to use silicon to keep bones and cartilage healthy.

# What Are Silica and Silicone?

The silicon compound used to make glass is called **silica**. Like sand, silica is made of silicon and oxygen. In fact, it is known as silica sand. Silica sand, however, is purer than the sand found on most beaches. Beach sand is a mix-

Quartz is the second most common mineral in Earth's crust.

ture of different silicates, including quartz, feldspar, and clay. Silica sand is mostly quartz. Silica sand is treated to remove the small amount of impurities it contains. The final product is almost pure quartz.

Silica is mixed with some other substances and then heated in a furnace to about 3,600° Fahrenheit (1,980° Celsius) for up to a day. The heat turns the mixture into glass. This glass is used to make windows,

The element boron is added to silica to make the heat-resistant glass used in science laboratories.

bottles, computer screens, and many other products. Adding the element lead to the silicate mixture makes glass that sparkles and is easy to engrave. This type of glass is called lead crystal. It is often used to make vases, decanters, and bowls.

An artist engraves a lead crystal vase.

Another group of silicon compounds are known as **silicones**. Unlike the silicon compounds you have read about so far, however, silicones are not found in nature. They are synthetic compounds. This means that they are made by humans and are never found in nature.

A silicone compound is made by joining silicon with oxygen to make a long chain, or backbone. Other

This play putty is a silicone compound.

elements are then added to this backbone.

Silicones have many uses. Some are used as sealants because they are water-resistant. Some are used as lubricants because they are greasy. Some are used in polishes because they pro-tect against spills. Some are used in shampoos because they make hair smooth and silky. When you consider all the household products that

People work in a factory that produces shampoo. The silicone in some shampoos helps make hair smooth.

contain silicone, it's no wonder that you can find silicon almost everywhere.

# Fixing Leaks

Experiment to see how well silicone works in sealing leaks. Ask an adult to use a large nail to poke a hole in the bottom of several empty aluminum cans. Plug one hole with a silicone sealer that you can get at a hardware store. Seal each of the other holes with household products, such as chewing gum, vegetable shortening, tape, and melted wax that is allowed to cool. Label each can so you know what you used to seal the hole. Place the cans in a basin or sink and fill them with water. Which seal allows the water to start leaking first? Is silicone the best sealer? Does silicone sealer still do a good job of sealing the leak if the water is hot?

# Fun Facts About Silicon

- Silicon that is almost 100 percent pure costs about $1,600 per pound.

- Silicon is obtained by heating sand along with the element carbon to about 4,000° Fahrenheit (2,200° C).

- Another silicon compound, commonly called water glass, is used to preserve eggs.

- Silicates make up the largest group of gemstones, including amethyst, opal, peridot, topaz, and zircon.

- The packets that come with new electronic devices, such as cameras, contain silica that absorbs moisture and prevents rust from forming.

# To Find Out More

To learn more about silicon, check out these additional sources.

Books

Llewellyn, Claire. **Glass.** Franklin Watts, 2001.

Oxlade, Chris. **How We Use Glass.** Raintree Steck-Vaughn, 2004

Thomas, Jens. **Silicon.** Benchmark Books, 2001.

Tocci, Salvatore. **The Periodic Table.** Children's Press, 2004.

## Organizations and Online Sites

### How Semiconductors Work

*http://science.howstuff works.com/diode1.htm*

Examine how silicon is arranged to make a crystal. You can also learn how silicon is "doped" with other elements to make it a conductor of electricity. Links explain the "doping" process and how semiconductors work.

### It's Elemental

*http://education.jlab.org/ itselemental/ele014.html*

Learn how silicon was first discovered. You can also check out some of silicon's properties, such as its melting and boiling points.

### Silicones

*http://chemcases.com/ silicon/sil13one.htm*

This site provides a list of the fifteen major uses of silicone, including medical products, paints, plastics, and food processing.

# Important Words

*compound* substance formed from the combination of two or more elements

*crystal* substance in which the building blocks, such as elements, are arranged in a specific ordered pattern

*element* building block of matter

*matter* stuff or material that makes up everything in the universe

*semiconductor* substance that acts like both a metal and a nonmetal

*silica* substance that is almost pure silicon and oxygen

*silicate* substance made of silicon, oxygen, and sometimes other elements

*silicone* substance that contains silicon, oxygen, and other elements and is made by humans (not found in nature)

# Index

# Meet the Author

Salvatore Tocci is a science writer who lives in East Hampton, New York, with his wife, Patti. He was a high school biology and chemistry teacher for almost thirty years. His books include a high school chemistry textbook and an elementary school book series that encourages students to perform experiments to learn about science.

9/21/05